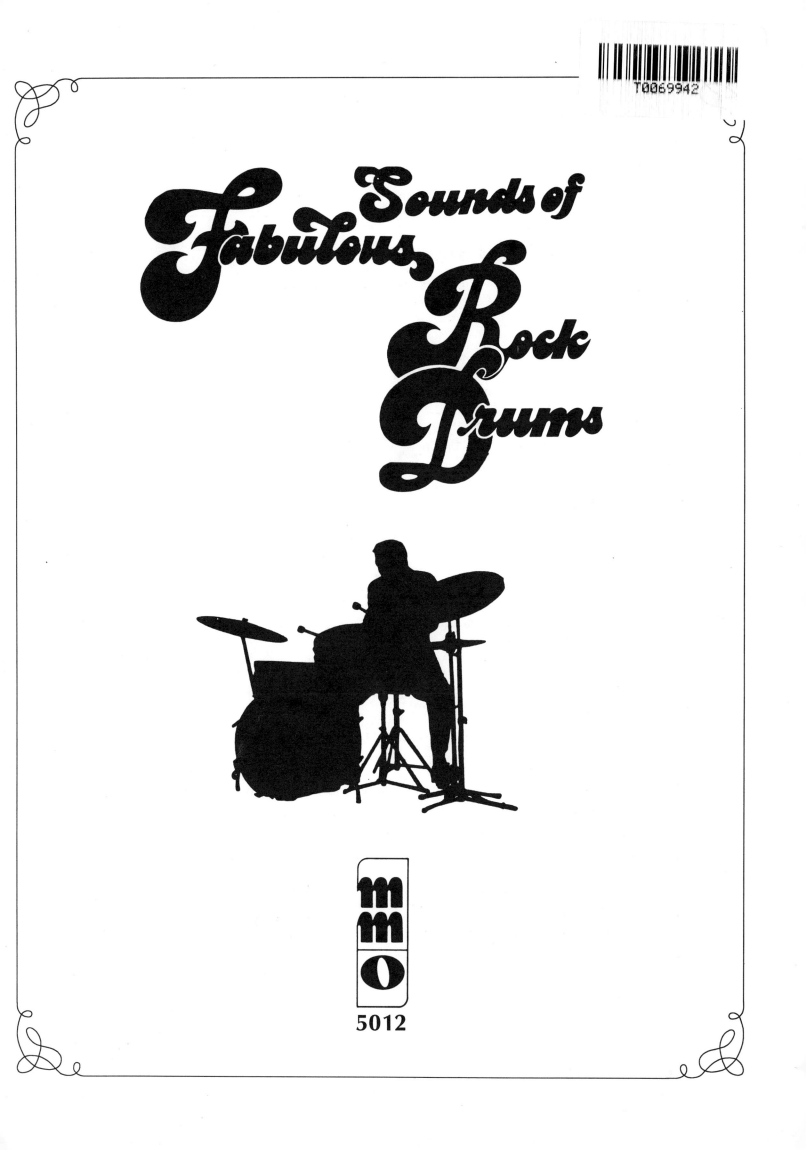

Sounds of Fabulous Rock Drums

mmo

5012

MMO

5012

Fabulous Sounds of Rock Drums
Conceived by Charles Perry

CONTENTS

GLOSSARY OF SYMBOLS AND TERMS

RH = right hand
Cym. = cymbal (top cymbal, unless stated otherwise)
BD = bass drum
hi-h = hi-hat
LT = large tom

TT = tom tom (strike either tom)
LH = left hand
SD = snare drum
ST = small tom
H to H = hand-to-hand sticking: R L R L etc.

= quarter-note on top cymbal

= quarter-note on hi-hat

= quarter-note on bass drum

= quarter note on snare drum
(this note is also used for tom toms)

= quarter rest (count but don't play rests)

= eighth rest (count but don't play)

= sixteenth rest (count but don't play)

> = accent mark: notes with accent marks above them are called accented notes. Such notes are struck harder than unaccented notes (notes not so marked.)

‖: :‖ = repeat sign:

the music between two such marks (double bars with dots alongside) is played twice. However, for the purpose of practice, the music between these double-bar marks may be played many times over.

- whole rest (black box above line)

- half rest (black bos below line)

This is a "repeat measure" meaning repeat the measure before it.

Cresendo mark: going from soft to loud.

Diminuendo (descrescendo) mark: going from loud to soft.

"Band" refers to a unit of grooves on the record. For example, on "pop" (commerical) records, each "band" (each unit of grooves) represents a separate tune. The bands on a record are sometimes referred to as "tracks." Here, the separate "bands" designate the recorded rhythms or the recorded rock group. Example: Band 1 consists of the narrator's dialogue over the recorded drummer's solo: Band 2 consists of narration and the properties of tone; and so forth.

FORM

By "form" we mean the structural design in musical composition; combining musical ideas into a unified whole; order and proportion in music; a mold or framework.

By the "rock form of drumming" we mean the structural design (mold; framework;) the order and proportion of rock drumming. Briefly, the particular way (the rock way) or combining musical ideas (rhythmic and tonal) into a unitied whole.

The two, the chorus form and rock drumming, go together: What the drummer plays is regulated by the continuity of the music – the parts and the whole of the chorus, the time signature, etc. Therefore, the figures, phrases and rhythmic and tonal climaxes conceived by the drummer are rleated to the two and four bar phrases, the eight and sixteen-measure period, the thirty-two bar tune (chorus), the twelve-bar blues chorus, the sixteen-bar chorus, or whatever it may be.

Here we are attempting to explain form structurally, to show how a composition (a tune) is constructed. Let's begin by defining the terms used in describing the parts of some of the elements that go into the making of a tune.

Figure: A short succession of musical notes which produces a *single impression.* A short, coherent group of tones or chords (where drumming is concerned, rhythmic patterns as well), which may grow into a phrase, a theme, or an entire composition.

A good example of a "figure" is the cymbal ride rhythm (used in jazz, rhythm and blues, and "commercial" dance music). Although it is written and counted at follows,

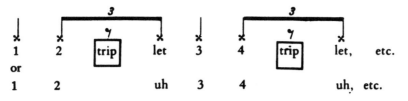

the "ear" is impressed with the singularity of a particular rhythmic sound, which may sound to some like Ding Ding Da Ding Ding Da, etc. This distinct rhythmic-sound unit forms a figure, in this case, a two-beat figure: it takes the place (the time unit) of two beats. Example:

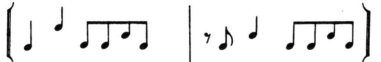

one beat + one beat = two beats of time value

Here are several of the "figures" used in this book: one beat + one beat = two beats   one beat + one beat = two beats

Phrase: A short musical thought at least two, but usually four measures in length which presents an independent, but incomplete, musical tought. It is like a phrase in speech that needs another phrase to complete the meaning. Note: The term phrase is also sometimes used to mean a short series or cluster of notes of less than two bars.

Here is an example of a two-bar rhythm phrase used in this book:

Period: The period is an independent musical thought consisting of two or more phrases which form a complete musical sentence. In popular music the period is usually eight or sixteen measures. The twelve-measure blues can be considered as a twelve-measure period, made up of three four-measure phrases.

SONG FORM

The thirty-two measure standard song (tune) and the twelve-measure blues are common forms in "pop" (popular) music – jazz, rock, rhythm & blues, etc.

The following is an analysis of the thirty-two measure chorus, in this case the A A B A form. (Each letter consists of eight measures).

The first letter A constitutes a period in which the main theme (the melody) is stated.

The letter B consists of a contrasting melodic period (theme) of eight measures which is inserted for the purpose of variety. (The balance of unity and variety is indispensable to music.)

This section, letter B, is termed the release (also called the bridge, middle or channel.)

The next section, which follows letter B, is the original letter A repeated, either in its exact form or, sometimes, in a modified form in order to complete the song.

A 8 measures theme	A 8 measures theme repeated	B 8 measures contrasting theme (release)	B 8 measures original theme repeated

This album contains both the twelve-bar blues and the thirty-two-bar chorus. ("measure" and "bar" are used interchangeably here)

Also, the at-home drummer is offered eight and sixteen-bar groupings as well as the twelve and thirty-two bar chorus to practice with.

THE METHOD OF GRIPPING AND MANIPULATING THE DRUM STICKS

RIGHT HAND: The stick is gripped between the inside of the thumb and the first joint (from the top) of the index finger; the remaining fingers are held around the stick (closed, but not tightly). The motion of the stroke is up and down. See illustrations "A" and "B". In "A" the stick is in an "up position"; in "B" it is in a "down position."

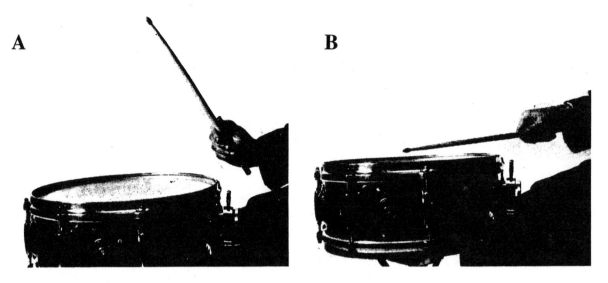

LEFT HAND: The student may use either the "traditional grip" (see illustrations "C" and "D") or the "matched grip" (also known as the "overhand grip") for the left hand.

TRADITIONAL GRIP: The stick is gripped in the crotch between the base of the thumb and the index finger; the index finger and middle finger are placed over the stick; the last two fingers are placed under the stick. The stick is gripped between base of thumb and index finger; the fingers support and help control the stick, but are not held too tightly. See illustrations "C" and "D". In "C" the stick is in an "up position"; in "D" it is in a "down position." The hand, wrist, and forearm turn together (rotate) as one unit (from the tips of the fingers to the elbow) making a rotating motion.

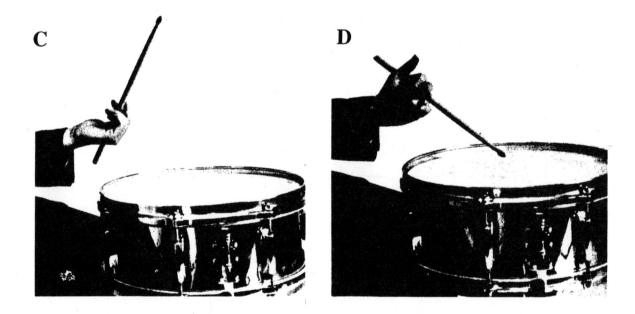

THE MATCHED GRIP: The left-hand grip is the very same at the right-hand grip. In other words, in the matched grip **both** hands are held identically (the left hand uses the right-hand grip). Therefore, follow the same instructions for the left hand as for the right hand when using the matched grip – Illustration E.

THE DRUM SET: TONE

Think of the drums and cymbals in terms of tone as well as rhythm. Why? Because the rhythms played by the drummer on the drum set are realized in sound – tone. Therefore, let's examine the properties of tone, which are:

Pitch – a high or low sound

Duration (length of note) – a short or long sound

Intensity – a hard or easy sound (touch); loud or soft; tense or loose

Timbre – the particular (characteristic) tone quality, such as snare drum tone, bass drum tone, tom tom tone, cymbal tone, etc.

Experiment by striking different drums and cymbals:

High sound – strike the small tom

Low sound – strike the large tom

Short sound – strike the center of the snare drum

Long sound – strike the cymbal

Loud sound – strike the snare drum hard

Soft sound – strike the snare drum softly

BAND 2: The Properties of Tone as applied to the Drum Set.

high sound – small tom

low sound – large tom

short sound – center of snare drum

long sound – cymbal

loud sound – snare drum struck hard

soft sound – snare drum struck softly

Let's continued with dynamics: A crescendo – going from soft to loud:

A dimineuendo – going from loud to soft:

ACCENTS: Accented notes are struck harder than unaccented note. [The following is an accent mark: >
Notes with accent marks above them are struck harder than unaccented notes (notes not so marked).]

Listen to the recorded drummer as he accents every other note – the "2" and "4". Count: 1 2 3 4 1 2 3 4:

 Two measures of quarter-notes on the snare drum.

The same accents played faster. Count: 1 2 3 4 1 2 3 4: (Recorded drummer plays four measures.)

To further explore the area of tone, listen to the recorded drummer play clockwise around the four drums, in this order – snare drum – small tom – large tom – bass drum.

The same played faster.

End of Band 2.

NOTE

The Left-handed Drummer: The material in this book was designed for the right-handed drummer. The left-handed drummer must, therefore, reverse the instructions for the hands and feet. Example: what is designated for the right hand, the left-handed drummer will play with the left hand. What is designated for the left hand, the left-handed drummer will play with the right hand. The same applies to the right and left foot.

Special Effect: For a special tonal effect, the hi-hat is sometimes used to make a clanging sound (open sound) rather than the usual short click sound. The purpose of this is to add a different tone color to the drum-set sound; to achieve a long sound instead of a short sound (chick sound). See section dealing with hi-hat.

THE RECORDED DRUMMER plays double bass drums on Band 1 and Band 21. He plays single bass drum on all of the other bands.

THE AT-HOME DRUMMER is invited to add to and embellish the rhythms in this book according to his own ability and ingenuity.

SOME of the sections in the arrangements which are marked "fill" are filled in by the recorded organ player or the guitar player. At such times, the at-home drummer may "fill," or continue playing a rhythm patterns, or lay out (not play). See section of book dealing with FILLS.

BEFORE attempting to play the "fill," the at-home drummer should first listen to the recorded drummer play the fills.

IN order to better analyze some of the rhythms, it might be a good idea for the at-home drummer to play the record at speed 16 (the very slow speed on the record player).

GENERALLY, the material in this book will require much practice to gain a high level of proficiency. This, of course, depends upon the individual drummer's ability.

COUNTING MEASURES OF RHYTHM: Count **1 2 3 4 2 2 3 4 3 2 3 4 4 2 3 4**, etc. or simply say the first number of each measure 1 _ _ _ 2 _ _ _ , etc. This is called consecutive counting.

THE FUNDAMENTAL RHYTHM STRUCTURE

The fundamental rhythm structure that is used to generate and "keep time" in the rock form of drumming is composed of these related parts – the rhythm of the top cymbal, the bass drum, the hi-hat, and the snare drum. The rhythms of the toms are then added, usually in the form of "fills", to this basic structure.

The harmonious blending of the cymbals and the drums will occur as the student's coordination and sense of time develop, and as he comprehends the interrelation of the parts as dominated by the character of the whole.

THE PARTS: The Cymbal Rhythm

The cymbal rhythm is played with a drum stick, held in the right hand, on the top cymbal or the hi-hat cymbals. [Left-handed drummers hold the drum stick with the left hand. See section – The Left-handed Drummer for further information.] Here, we shall play it on the top cymbal. The hi-hat will be studied at a later point in this book.

REVIEW: The method of gripping and manipulating the stick with the right hand is described in the section The Method of Gripping and Manipulating The Drum Sticks.

The right-hand motion is up-and-down. The "bead" (front tip of stick) strikes the cymbal and rebounds (bounces up) about an inch or so, depending on the power of the stroke.

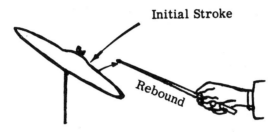

The height of the cymbal stroke varies. Low strokes for soft playing; high strokes for loud playing.

Remember – the stroke (called tap stroke) rebounds off the cymbal making a **single** sound (ding sound). **Don't** press the stick against cymbal in attempting to make a stroke!

Ultimately, the drummer may regulate the height (stick level) of the strokes as he sees fit.

Although the basic rock cymbal rhythm consists of straight-eighth notes – the straight-eight cymbal rhythm – its interpretation is left to the individual drummer. [The other rock cymbal rhythms will be taken up at a later point.] It is a very personalized element of drumming and no single interpretation can suffice for all drummers in all situations. The feeling, touch, and sound vary among drummers.

Furthermore, in the course of a performance it may be played in several ways, depending upon the tempo, the characteristics of the music, and the mood of the drummer.

The numerical device of notating the straight-eight cymbal rhythm serves to approximate the division of the notes. It does not tell all there is to the execution and interpretation of the cymbal rhythm. The drummer must translate these mute markings into meaningful rhythm and sound.

For example, the drummer may give the cymbal rhythm a literal interpretation; playing it exactly as written – no dynamics, no coloring, etc.:

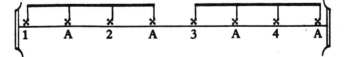

Note: In drum music, the capital A is pronounced AN or AND

However, he may also play it with light, or strong, accents on numbers, as follows:

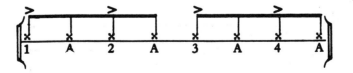

In so doing, he may even "throw away" the A's. That is, he may give particular emphasis to the number 1 2 3 4 while barely striking the A's, thereby causing the A's to be almost inaudible. Also, some drummers play "up on the note" (on top of the beat), whereas other drummers prefer to "lay back" (a feeling of delaying the time).

At this point, the object is to play the straight-eighth cymbal rhythm; to experience the playing of it, and then to join it to the other parts of the basic time structure. Later, we will deal with the various other rock cymbal rhythms.

If the student so desires, he may substitute the straight-four cymbal rhythm for the straight-eighth rhythm. The straight-four cymbal is also a basic rhythm and ultimately the student must be able to use either of these two cymbal rhythms in conjunction with the snare drum, bass drum, and hi-hat rhythms.

The straight-four cymbal rhythm consists of quarter notes:

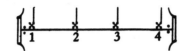

Stroking the Cymbal Rhythm: The hand-stick motion commonly used in playing the cymbal rhythm is the up-and-down motion. However, the side-to-side motion is also used by some drummers.

straight-to-side motion: ↕

side-to-side motion: ⤵

IMPORTANT: The cymbal rhythm may be played either on the top cymbal or the hi-hat.

When the cymbal rhythm is played on closed hi-hats, the hi-hats remain closed (shut); they do not play (chick) on the two and four.

However, the cymbal rhythm may be played on the hi-hats while they open and close on the two and four.

Ultimately, the dummer may use the hi-hat in any way that enhances the over-all rhythm and tonal effect.

Notice that on this record the top cymbal and the hi-hat are used for the cymbal rhythm.

BAND 3: CYMBAL RHYTHMS: The straight-eighth cymbal rhythm played on the top cymbal.
Count 1 A 2 A 3 A 4 A:

RH on top cymbal
One measure of
8th notes.

The same rhythm played in a faster tempo. Count: 1 A 2 A 3 A 4 A: (recorded drummer plays two measures)

The straight-eighth cymbal rhythm with accents on the 1 2 3 4.
Count: 1 A 2 A 3 A 4 A:

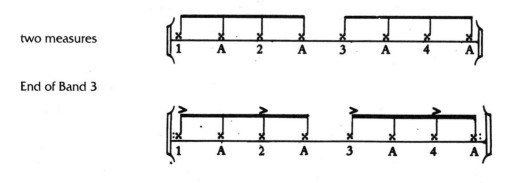

two measures

End of Band 3

THE PARTS: The Bass Drum

There are several ways of manipulating the bass drum pedal. The first way has the entire foot, both the ball and the heel, resting on the foot plate of the pedal. The pedal is motivated by the foot, with the ankle serving as the pivotal point (see illustration A). This is the method used by most swing, dance band, and jazz drummers.

Another way of playing the bass drum foot pedal consists of only the ball of the foot resting on the foot plate, with the heel held approximately an inch or more off the plate suspended in the air (see illustration B). The pedal can be motivated by the foot and leg together as one unit, moving up and down in unison (the way it is commonly done by rock drummers) or it can be manipulated by the foot alone, with the ankle serving as the pivotal point.

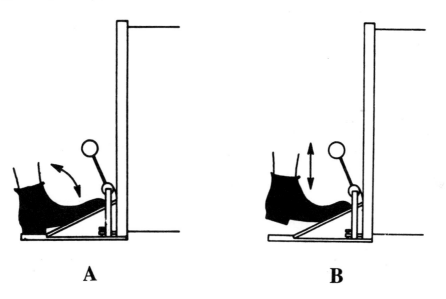

A   B

The complexity and/or loud volume of some rock drumming requires greater definition and loudness of the bass drum than the steady four-to-the-bar (or two-to-the-bar) of swing or dance drumming.

Most rock drummers find it easier to do the job with the leg and foot moving up and down together as a unit, particularly when playing loudly, rather than with the foot alone. The complex rhythms, etc. particularly when loudness is not required, are usually best accomplished by using the foot alone, with the ankle serving as the pivotal point.

All of these methods of playing the foot pedal have merit. Therefore, it isn't a matter of one method being better than the other, but rather of deciding which of these is most suitable for you. Practice the different ways described here, then make your choice. Eventually, why not be able to play several ways?

A word of caution: Regardless of which way you practice, be careful not to fatigue the muscles of your foot and leg. When you begin to tire, stop. Rest. Don't resume playing until your muscles are thoroughly rested.

Note: the right-handed drummer is usually right-footed, whereas the left-handed drummer is usually left-footed. The right-footed drummer plays the bass drum with his right foot.

BAND 4: THE BASS DRUM: The right foot plays the bass drum on the "1" and "3" of the measure. This is called playing the bass drum in "2".

four measures
of quarters (and rests)
on the bass drum

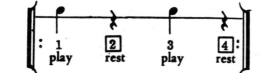

Note: Count, but don't play numbers in squares. The "2" and "4" are quarter rests. Count, but don't play on the rests.

THE PARTS: The Left Hand

In discussing the part of the left hand in the fundamental rhythm structure, we have included the rim shot as well as the tap. Both have their place as part of the left-hand rhythm pattern.

The tap and the rim shot have been recorded so that the at-home drummer can differentiate between the two.

THE TAP

Almost all of what the drummer plays is done with "taps." The remainder consists of buzzes (which go into making closed rolls), and rim shots of different sorts.

The at-home drummer may use either the traditional left-hand grip (illustration D), or the left-hand matched grip (illustrations E and F).

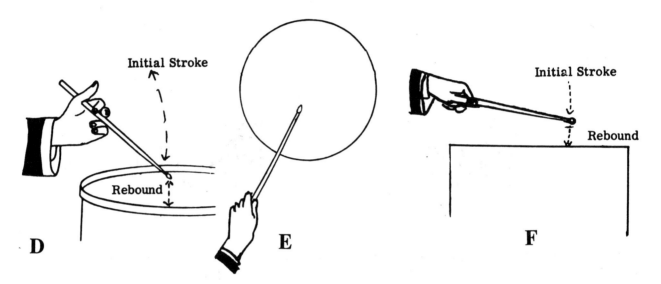

REVIEW the left-hand stroke – see section - The Method of Gripping and Manipulating the Drum Sticks in the forward section of the book, page 6.

When making the tap with the left-hand traditional grip, the wrist and forearm turn together (rotate) as one unit from the tips of the fingers to the elbow.

The stick (arm and hand together) rotates up in preparation for the coming tap stroke, and then rotates downward in making the tap stroke. The "bead" of the stick (front tip of stick) strikes the center of the drum head and rebounds (bounces up) about an inch or so, depending on the power of the stroke. The tap stroke may rebound higher if the drummer so desires.

When making the left-hand tap with the matched grip an up-and-down motion is used. The arm remains stationary; it **doesn't** rotate; only the wrist makes a motion (up-and-down; the wrist **doesn't** rotate)! The up-and-down wrist motion is also known as a "wrist break." In other words, the wrist "breaks" in making the up-and-down motion, but the arm remains relatively still.

THE RIM SHOT

The Rim shot is a tonal ingredient found in all drumming that has to do with the drum set, whether the music is jazz, rock, or whatever. But in much of rock it occupies a special place: it is one of the major parts of the fundamental rhythm structure (the time-keeping and time-generating mechanism). When used in this context the rim shot is made with the left-hand stick on the snare drum, solidly emphasized on the **two** and **four** of the measure (these **two** and **four** rim shots apply to music in four-four time).

In making the rim shot, the drum stick simultaneously strikes the rim and the drum head. [This applies to rim shorts made with either the right hand or left hand. It also holds true whether the drummer uses the traditional grip or the matched grip with the left hand.]

In music notation, the letters R.S. stand for rim shot.

Not all forms and styles of rock, however, have heavy rim shots on the "2" and "4" as part of the time-keeping and time-generating device. Remember, what comes under the broad heading of rock is diversified; in the subdivisions of rock, the branches spread in many directions. Nevertheless, in much of rock, the heavy "afterbeat" (the "2" & "4"), which is best stated by rim shots, is a major element of the fundamental rhythm structure. Even among those drummers who employ a "busy" left hand (the drummers who add extra notes to the framework of the two and four), the emphasized rim shots on "2" and "4" are commonplace.

Rim shots, of course, are also used in drum fills and drum solos, and are made with either hand.

Another rhythmic-tonal effect used in rock drumming is the "click" rim stroke made with the left hand. This too is used as an afterbeat (on the "2" and "4") in the fundamental rhythmic structure.

The drum stick is gripped with the index finger and the thumb; the other fingers and the heel of the hand rest on the drum head; the butt end (tail end) of the stick extends over the rim, while the front end (the "bead" of the stick) rests on the drum head. In other words, the drum stick is held backwards. The stroke is made with an up-and-down motion. See illustration:

"click"
stick &
rim effect

The tap, the rim shot, and the "click" rim sound are recorded here in that order:

SNARE DRUM TAP: The left hand plays **taps** on the snare drum on the "2" and "4". Count: 1 2 3 4 1 2 3 4:

LH
on
SD
two measures
quarters and
quarter rests

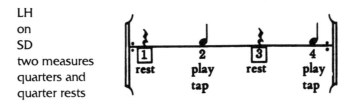

THE RIM SHOT: The left hand plays rim shots on the snare drum on the "2" and "4". Count: 1 2 3 4 1 2 3 4

LH
on
SD
two measures

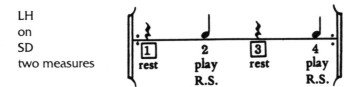

R.S. = rim shot

THE "CLICK" RIM SOUND: The left hand plays the "click" rim sound on the snare drum on the "2" and "4": Count: 1 2 3 4 1 2 3 4:

LH
on
SD
two
measures

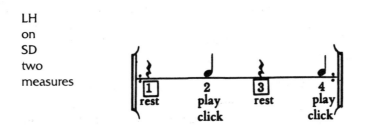

THE PARTS: The Hi-Hat

Note: the right-footed drummer (drummer who plays the bass drum with his right foot) plays the hi-hat with his left foot.

There are several ways of playing the hi-hat. One is the "rocking motion": The entire foot rests on the foot plate of the hi-hat pedal. The front part of the foot (ball and toes) snaps down hard on the "2" and "4" (afterbeat); the heel is slightly raised when the front part of the foot snaps down, thereby causing the heel to tap as it returns to the foot plate on the "1" and "3." Note: the front part of the foot must remain down on the pedal at all times so that the hi-hat cymbals remain shut during the interim between beats. If the cymbals were to open while the heel was tapping on the "1" and "3" it would result in a long, clanging sound instead of a short "chick" sound. The hi-hat gets a crisp, distinct "chick" sound. See illustrations "A" and "B".

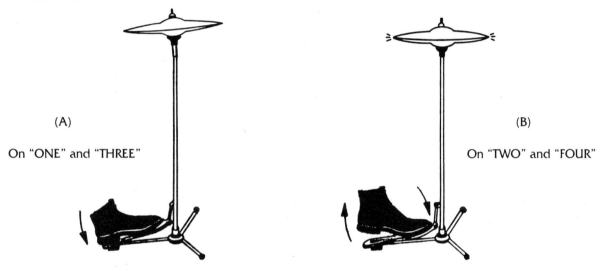

(A)

On "ONE" and "THREE"

(B)

On "TWO" and "FOUR"

Another method of playing the hi-hat is knows as the "dancing motion": keep the front part (ball and toes) of the foot down on the pedal; the heel of the foot is suspended in mid-air about an inch or more above the foot plate. The pedal is manipulated by the foot and leg together moving up and down as one unit.

Either of the methods described may be used to manipulate the hi-hat pedal.

THE HI-HAT: The left foot plays the hi-hat on the "2" and "4" producing a "chick" sound. Count: 1 2 3 4 1 2 3 4:

      hi-hat
      two measures

For special tonal effect, the drummer may make a clanging (or chinging) sound with the hi-hat. This is done by making a **sudden** snapping motion with the foot causing the hi-hat cymbals to **suddenly strike** each other and **instantly** upon contact separate again! Upon completion of this effect the cymbals are in an open position (parted position). See following illustration.

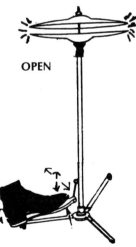

OPEN

BAND 5: JOINING THE PARTS: Let's begin by joining two parts – the straight-eighth cymbal rhythm; the bass drum on "1" and "3". Count: 1 A 2 A 3 A 4 A 1 A 2 A 3 A 4 A:

RH on top cymbal
two measures

BD

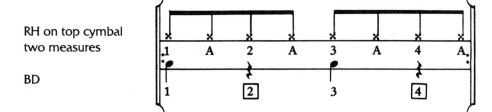

Notes joined by arrows are struck simultaneously (played together).

This time, combine the straight-eighth cymbal rhythm with snare drum taps on the "2" and "4". Count: 1 A 2 A 3 A 4 A 1 A 2 A 3 A 4 A:

RH on top cymbal
two measures
LH on SD

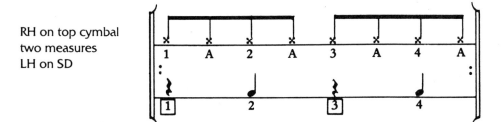

Note: Where it is practical, the **actual** sound of the rhythm pattern will be used in counting. But where the rhythm is too complex or too fast for clear verbalization, straight counting, such as 1 2 3 4 or 1 A 2 A 3 A 4 A, will be used in it's place. Remember – these ways of counting are **suggestions:** You **may** count in the way which is best suited to you.

Here we combine the bass drum on the 1 and 3 with the hi-hat on 2 and 4. The tonal effect is boom chick boom chick. Count: 1 2 3 4 Boom Chick Boom Chick:

BD
&
Hi-hat
4 measures

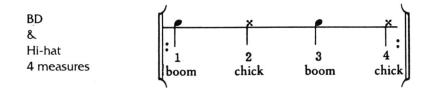

Note: This rhythm pattern (the boom chick boom chick) may be written as shown above – the bass drum and hi-hat notes written along side each other, on the same line of the staff – or it may be written as follows, the bass drum notes above; the hi-hat notes beneath:

BD

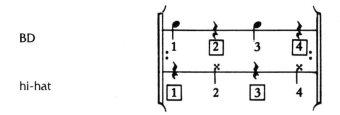

hi-hat

Regardless of which of the two ways this rhythm is written, it is played the same way. In either case the bass drum plays on the "1" and "3", while the hi-hat plays on the "2" and "4" – boom chick boom chick.

BAND 6: JOINING THREE PARTS: Now we will join three parts – the straight-eighth cymbal rhythm, the bass drum on 1 and 3, the hi-hat on 2 and 4. Count 1 A 2 A 3 A 4 A:

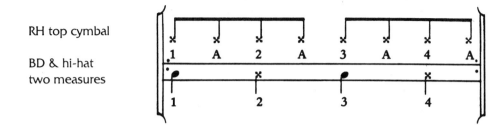

RH top cymbal

BD & hi-hat
two measures

Another combination of three parts consists of the straight-eighth cymbal rhythm, the snare drum on 2 and 4, the 1 and 3 of the bass drum. Count: 1 A 2 A 3 A 4 A 1 A 2 A 3 A 4 A:

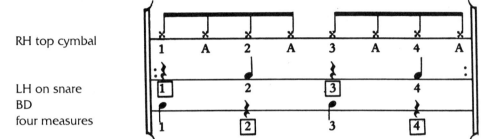

RH top cymbal

LH on snare
BD
four measures

JOINING FOUR PARTS: For the first time we will join the four parts of the fundamental rhythm pattern – the straight-eighth cymbal rhythm, the bass drum on 1 and 3, the snare drum on 2 and 4, and the hi-hat on 2 and 4. Count: 1 A 2 A 3 A 4 A 1 A 2 A 3 A 4 A:

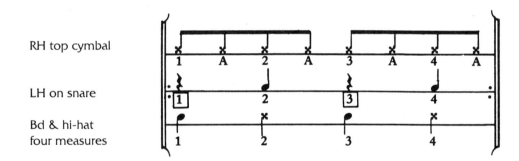

RH top cymbal

LH on snare

Bd & hi-hat
four measures

The same rhythm played faster. Count 1 A 2 A 3 A 4 A 1 A 2 A 3 A 4 A: (Recorded drummer plays four measures)

If the at-home drummer encounters difficulty coordinating the four parts, he should at first play only three parts – the top cymbal, snare drum, and hi-hat. Then, **while** in the process of playing the three parts, he should add the hi-hat to the parts he is already playing. If this doesn't work for him, he may try playing the snare drum, bass drum, and hi-hat. Then, in the course of playing these parts, he should add the top cymbal rhythm.

Remember, if one approach doesn't work for you, try another. The aid of a good teacher can help considerably in dealing with such problems.

End of Band 6.

PRACTICING WITH THE RECORDED GROUP
(The recorded group: organ, bass, and guitar,
plus drums, begins at band 7)

The at-home drummer may play the preceding rhythm pattern with the recorded group. He may even find that he is able to play a rhythm of his own making, or one that he has picked up from listening to records. Or, if he likes, he may use the rhythm that the recorded drummer plays with the group.

However, in the event that the at-home drummer is not ready at this time to play a complete rhythm pattern with the recorded group, he may, instead, play the parts separately from one another. For example, he may play the cymbal alone, or, the cymbal and snare drum together; or the cymbal, snare drum, and bass drum, and so forth.

Concerning the fills: If he can, the at-home drummer may play the same fills as the recorded drummer. Or, he may play fills of his own making. If he can't do either, he should drop out (not play) during the open spots, leaving them to be filled by the recorded organ or guitar; or he may continue playing the rhythm pattern throughout the open places (where the fills are normally played).

Because the level of proficiency differs among the at-home drummers, there is no set of rules that applies to everyone in every situation. The at-home drummer, or his instructor, should make the proper decisions as to what to do where.

It is suggested that the at-home drummer first listen to the recorded drummer play with the group before attempting to do so himself.

[See Glossary of Terms and Symbols for additional information – ways of counting measures of rhythm, repeat measures, etc.]

NOTE: At this point, some of the notation (the way in which the rhythms are written) differs from the preceding notation (written music). The author feels that different situations call for different notations. This is particularly true with complex rhythm patterns, where the simpler the notation the better. (The complex rhythms occur later in the book.) Too many "rests" written across the page tend to confuse rather than clarify. The following way of writing the cymbal, snare drum, and bass drum eliminates the need for some of the usual "rest marks" (notation):

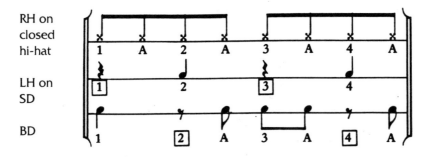

Note: The same markings can be used for top cymbal or closed hi-hat, as shown above. This occurs when the stick plays the cymbal rhythm on the hi-hat instead of the top cymbal.

Here is the same rhythm pattern written differently:

Remember – regardless of which of the two ways the above rhythm is written, it is played the same!

In Band 7 a written out sixteen-bar drum part is played. The first measure shows the rhythm played by the recorded drummer. Measures two through seven are repeated measures – meaning that the first measure (the rhythm pattern is played six more times, totaling seven measures in all. Then, the drummer plays the first beat (the 1) of the eighth measure, where this rhythm pattern stops. As you can see, beats 2 3 4 are written as quarter rests; but the word "fill" is written above these rests. This means that the drummer should fill in the remainder of the eighth measure (the 2 3 4) as he sees fit (and play the fill of his choice). However, since this is a "learning situation," the at-home drummer has several choices open to him, as discussed in the preceding paragraphs (PRACTICING WITH THE RECORDED GROUP). If necessary, please read these paragraphs **again!**

The ninth measure indicated "play rhythm pattern," meaning that the at-home drummer may play the rhythm pattern of his choice. Normally, in drum-chart notation, either the drum rhythm would be written out or the words "play time" would appear. But since the term "rhythm pattern" has been used throughout this instruction book, the author feels that it should be used instead of "play time." As used in this book, therefore, the terms "play rhythm pattern" and "play time" mean the same thing.

Usually, but not always, the written drum rhythm is offered merely as a "suggested rhythm," leaving it to the individual drummer to supply the appropriate rhythm. And where "play time" appears, of course, the choice of the appropriate rhythm is left to the drummer.

In the sixteenth measure, the at-home drummer may end with the group on the first beat (the 1 of the sixteenth measure) or he may end by playing a "fill" through the last beats (the 2 3 4) of the measure.

BAND 7: Now we have a recorded group for the at-home drummer to practice with. However, before attempting to play along with them, he should first read carefully and follow the practice plan in the book section of this album (as explained in the preceding paragraphs, Practicing With The Recorded Group).

The recorded format is as follows:

The group plays an eight-measure period twice, sixteen measures in all. The first eight measures are with the recorded drummer; the last eight measures are minus the recorded drummer. Count: 1 2 3 4:

Finally, the group, minus the drums, plays sixteen measures in a brighter tempo. Count: 1 2 3 4:
(Use the same written format as shown above; the format for the slower tempo.)
End of band 7.

Here we begin a new series of rhythm patterns.

BAND 8: In the following pattern, we add an eighth note to the boom chick of the bass drum and hi-hat. Count: 1 2 A 3 4 boom chick boom boom chick.

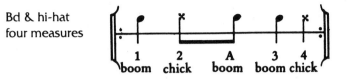

Bd & hi-hat
four measures

The same rhythm played faster. Count: 1 2 A 3 4 boom chick boom chick. (The recorded drummer plays four measures.)

The same bass drum and hi-hat rhythm, add the snare drum on 2 and 4. Count: 1 2 A 3 4 1 2 A 3 4:

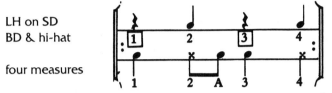

LH on SD
BD & hi-hat

four measures

The same rhythm in a faster tempo. Count: 1 2 A 3 4 1 2 A 3 4: (The recorded drummer plays four measures.)

And now, add the straight-eighth cymbal rhythm. Count: 1 A 2 A 3 A 4 A 1 A 2 A 3 A 4 A:

RH on
Top Cymbal

LH on SD

BD & hi-hat
four measures

Play the same rhythm faster. Count: 1 A 2 A 3 A 4 A 1 A 2 A 3 A 4 A: (Recorded drummer plays four measures.)

BAND 9: Once again we have the recorded group. This time the music consists of a twelve-measure chorus, the blues, played twice – twenty-four measures in all. Let me remind the drummer at home that all the rhythms he has learned so far should be practiced with the group.

First, the group plays the first chorus with the recorded drummer; then, the second chorus is played minus the recorded drummer. Count: 1 2 3 4:

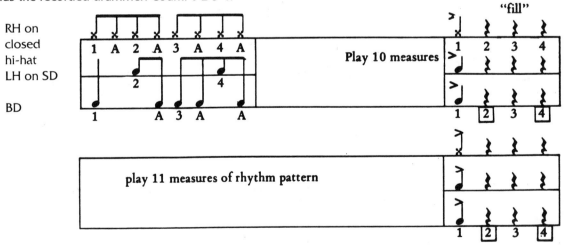

RH on
closed
hi-hat
LH on SD

BD

"fill"

Play 10 measures

play 11 measures of rhythm pattern

The at-home drummer may end on the first beat of the twenty-fourth measure (the 1) or he may end by playing a fill.

Next, the group, minus the recorded drummer, plays twenty four measures in a brighter tempo. (No verbal count here; instead the recorded drummer gives a "stick count-off": He taps one stick agains the other on 1 2 3 4.)

(Use the same written format as shown above; the format for the slower blues.)

End of Band 9.

BAND 10: At this point, we will return to the previous bass drum and hi-hat rhythm, to which we add still another eighth-note. Count: 1 2 A 3 4 A boom chick boom boom chick boom:

BD &
hi-hat
four measures

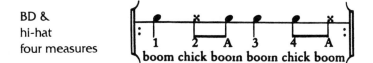

The same rhythm played faster. Count: 1 2 A 3 4 A boom chick boom boom chick boom. Recorded drummer plays four measures.

To the same rhythm, add the straight-eighth cymbal rhythm: the snare drum on 2 and 4. Count: 1 2 A 3 4 A 1 2 A 3 4 A:

RH on
Top Cymbal

LH on SD
BD &
hi-hat
four measures

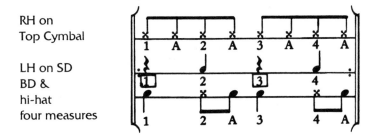

The same rhythm faster. Count 1 2 A 3 4 A 1 2 A 3 4 A; Recorded drummer plays four measures.

Here we have a variation of the previous bass drum and hi-hat rhythm. Count: boom chick boom–boom chick boom boom chick boom–boom chick boom:

BD & hi-hat
four measures

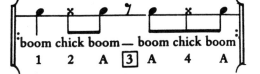

The same rhythm played faster. Count: boom chick boom–boom chick boom boom chick boom–boom chick boom. Recorded drummer plays four measures.

Add the straight-eighth cymbal rhythm, with the snare drum on 2 and 4. You may count as you wish or as follows. Count: 1 A 2 A 3 A 4 A 1 A 2 A 3 A 4 A:

RH on Top Cymbal

LH on SD

BD & hi-hat
four measures

The same rhythm played faster. Count: 1 A 2 A 3 A 4 A 1 A 2 A 3 A 4 A. Recorded drummer plays four measures.

A TWO-MEASURE PATTERN: In forming a two-measure pattern, we combine the two preceding bass drum and hi-hat rhythms. Count: boom chick boom boom chick boom boom chick boom–boom chick boom:

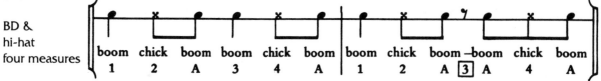

The same rhythm played faster. Count: boom chick boom boom chick boom boom chick boom–boom chick boom. Recorded drummer plays four measures.

To the same rhythm pattern, add the straight-eighth cymbal rhythm and the snare drum on 2 and 4. Count as you wish or as follows. Count: 1 A 2 A 3 A 4 A 1 A 2 A 3 A 4 A:

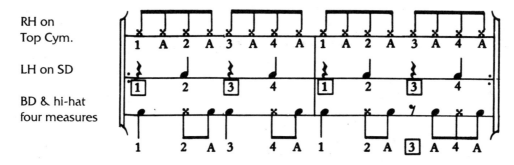

The same rhythm is a faster tempo. Count: 1 A 2 A 3 A 4 A 1 A 2 A 3 A 4 A. Recorded drummer plays four measures.

End of Band 10.

BAND 11: The group, minus the drums, plays sixteen measures in a slow tempo. The at-home drummer should play along using any of the rhythms of Band 10. (No verbal count-off; instead, stick count-off on 1 2 3 4:)

Play a seven-measure rhythm pattern: you may fill in on the eighth measure – it's left open for a drum fill. Again play seven measures of a rhythm pattern; stop on the first beat of measure 8 or play fill through measure 8 (marked measure 16 on the following written drum part).

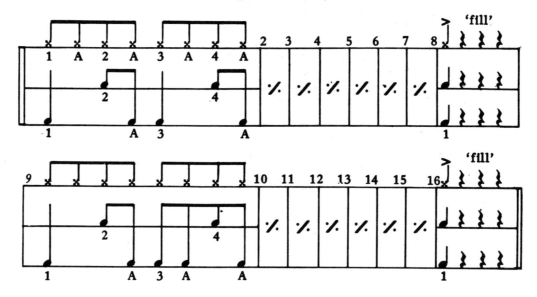

Now in a faster tempo, the group plays sixteen measures with drums, followed by sixteen measures minus drums. In all, we have a thirty-two bar chorus in the style of folk rock.

Upon completion of chorus, the music fades out.

Again we have a stick count-off. Sticks on 1 2 3 4:

Play 7 measures rhythm. You may use above rhythm (preceding drum part); any rhythm of Band 10; or rhythm of your choice.	one measure fill

Play 7 measures rhythm.	one measure fill

Play 8 measures You may play fill in measure eight	Play 8 measures—then music fades out

BAND 12: Here we have a new pattern combining quarters and eighths, played on the bass drum and snare. The snare plays on the 2 and 4. Count: 1 2 3 A 4 A 1 2 3 A 4 A:

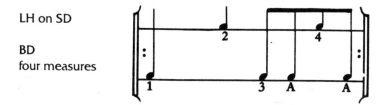

The same rhythm played brighter. Count: 1 2 3 A 4 A 1 2 3 A 4 A. Recorded drummer plays four measures.

Now add the straight-eighth cymbal rhythm; the hi-hat on 2 and 4. Count: 1 2 3 A 4 A 1 2 3 A 4 A:

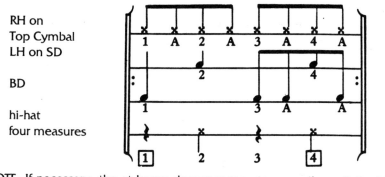

NOTE: If necessary, the at-home drummer may temporarily omit the hi-hat. That is, he may practice the top cymbal, snare drum and bass drum without the hi-hat. Then, finally, he may add the hi-hat when he has become proficient in playing the cymbal, snare drum and bass drum parts. This applies to all patterns which include the hi-hat rhythm.

Now we add an eighth on the '1' of the precediing bass drum and snare drum in rhythm. Count: 1 A 2–3 A 4 A 1 A 2–3 A 4 A:

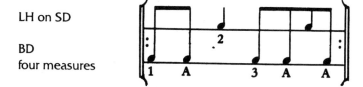

The same rhythm played faster. Count 1 A 2 3 A 4 A 1 A 2 3 A 4 A. Recorded drummer plays four measures.

Let's add the cymbal rhythm and the hi-hat. Count 1 A 2 A 3 A 4 A 1 A 2–3 A 4 A:

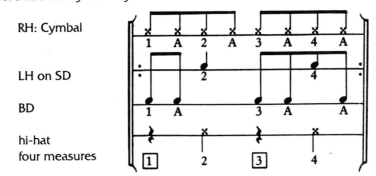

The same rhythm faster. Count: 1 A 2 A 3 A 4 A 1 A 2–3 A 4 A. Recorded drummer plays four measures.   End of Band 12.

SIDE B

BAND 13: here is a two-bar pattern divided between the bass drum and the snare. The snare plays on 2 and 4. Count as you wish or, as follows: Count: 1 A 2 A 3 A 4 A 1 A 2 A 3 A 4 A:

The same rhythm played faster. Count: 1 A 2 A 3 A 4 A 1 A 2 A 3 A 4 A. Recorded drummer plays four measures.

To the same rhythm, add cymbal eighths and the hi-hat on 2 and 4. Count: 1 A 2 A 3 A 4 A 1 A 2 A 3 A 4 A:

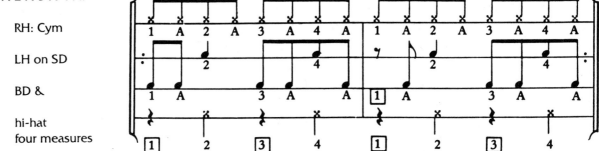

Same rhythm played faster. Count 1 A 2 A 3 A 4 A 1 A 2 A 3 A 4 A. Recorded drummer plays four measures.   End of Band 13.

BAND 14: The group, minus drums, plays twelve measures. The drummer at home accompanies the group with the rhythms of Bands 12 and 13. Count: 1 2 3 4:

Play eleven measures of rhythm pattern and end with one beat on the 1 of measure twelve; or you may play a fill through measure twelve.

Play eleven measures rhythm pattern	may play "fill" here (measure twelve)

The group, still minus drums, plays twenty-four measures in a slightly brighter tempo. The at-home drummer plays along with the rhythm of his choice. Count: 1 2 3 4:

Play eleven measures rhythm pattern	may play "fill" one measure (measure twelve)

Play eleven measures rhythm pattern	play one beat only of this measure

End of Band 14.

THE DRUM FILL

Open spots in songs may be filled in by an instrumentalists or a singer. When the drummer fills in the open space, it is called a "drum fill." In other words, the tonal-rhythmic pattern used to fill the open space **is** the drum fill, whether it is half a beat, one beat, two beats, or longer. Generally, the fill is about two beats.

A fill of one measure in length is also called a one bar solo, or a solo-fill. In this situation, the terms are interchangeable.

Anything of two or four measures is called a short solo (two or four-bar solo).

The drummer fills the open spaces in the arrangements or melody **only** when the open space is suitable for a drum fill. If the open space was made to be filled in by another instrument, the drummer may continue playing his regular time-keeping pattern without making a fill. He may, however, add his own fill to that of the other instrument or singer. In such a situation, what the drummer plays can become so conjoined with what is played by the other instrument or singer that there emerges a single fill-in partnership. The drums then are more than supporting or complementary. Actually, the drummer is in "conversation" with the soloist, in part providing responses, in part leading the conversation. Usually, but not always, the other "voice" (the other instrument or singer) remains the dominant member of the fill-in partnership. This is particularly true in the case of a vocal fill (one made by the singer).

In the first example, we have a two-beat fill (the fill takes the space of two beats of time value) beginning on the third beat of the measure. The fill figure consists of an eighth-note followed by two sixteenth notes.

The actual completion of the fill takes place on the first beat – the one – of the following measure:

BAND 15: THE DRUM FILL: Here we have a two-beat drum fill played on the third and fourth beats of the measure. Count: 1 A 2 A 3 A 4 A 1 A 2 A 3 A 4 A:

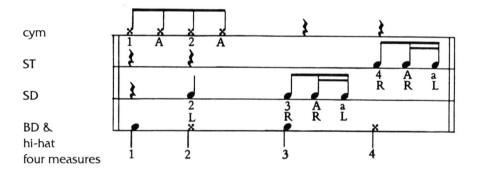

Note: The at-home drummer may change the bass drum and hi-hat rhythm if he so desires. He may, if he likes, play eighth-notes on the bass drum.

This time we have a one-measure fill. It is preceded by one measure of a rhythm pattern. In all, we have a two-measure phrase consisting of measures 1 and 2. (Play the bass drum and hi-hat rhythm of your choice.) Count: 1 A 2 A 3 A 4 A 1 A 2 A 3 A 4 A:

The second measure – the "fill":

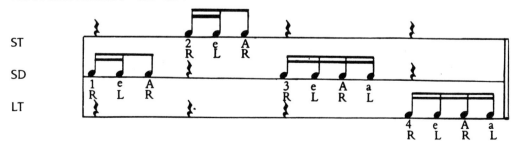

four measures in all, including rhythm patterns.

Now the recorded drummer plays the same fill, followed by a similar fill, with the group. Stick count-off on 1 2 3 4:

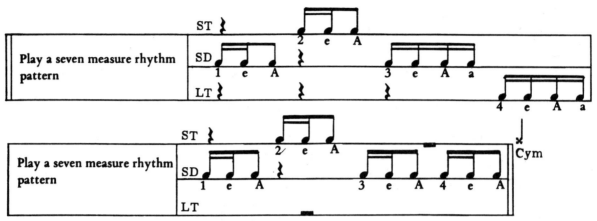

The recorded drummer plays a "fill" with the group in the eighth measure of the music. The at-home drummer is invited to try his hand at playing this fill or one of his own fills at the end of the music, the sixteenth measure. Count: 1 2 3 4:

Remember – the at-home drummer may end with the group on the first beat of the sixteenth measure, or he may end by playing a fill through the remainder of the sixteenth measure.

Here we have two one-measure fills in the eighth and sixteenth measures of the music. Listen carefully, read the music, then give it a try. Sick count-off on 1 2 3 4:

End of Band 15.

BAND 16: In preparation for some of the forthcoming rhythms, the at-home drummer will first practice two parts, the right hand and the left hand. (When he is able to play these two parts, he may add the bass drum and hi-hat.) Count: 1 A 2 A 3 A 4 A:

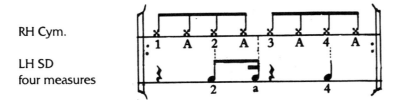

RH Cym.

LH SD
four measures

Notice that whereas the 2 and 4 of the snare drum coincides with the 2 and 4 of the cymbal rhythm, the "a" of the snare drum falls between the "A" and the "3" of the cymbal rhythm. The broken lines show the relationship of the snare drum rhythm to the cymbal rhythm.

The same rhythm played faster. Count 1 A 2 A 3 A 4 A 1 A 2 A 3 A 4 A. Recorded drummer plays four measures.

Let's try the bass drum and left hand together before joining the four parts. Count: 1 A 2–a3 A 4 A 1 A 2–a3 A 4 A:

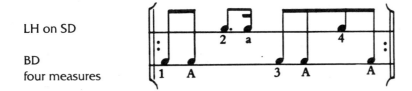

LH on SD

BD
four measures

The drummer may now join the four parts – the cumbal, the snare, the bass drum, and the hi-hat rhythm. Count: 1 A 2–a3 A 4 A 1 A 2–a3 A 4 A:

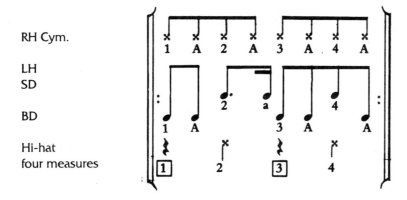

RH Cym.

LH
SD

BD

Hi-hat
four measures

We will add a sixteenth-note on the "e," between the "3" and the "A" of the bass drum and left-hand rhythm. Count: 1 A 2–a3e A 4 A 1 2–a3e A 4 A:

LH
SD

BD

four measures

Add the cymbal and hi-hat to the same rhythm. Count 1 A 2–a3e A 4 A 1 A 2–a3e A 4 A:

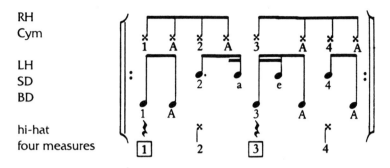

Let's add still another sixteenth-note, this time on the "a" after the last "A" of the measure. Count: 1 A 2–a3e A 4 Aa 1 A 2–a3e A 4 Aa:

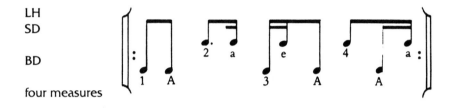

Now add the cymbal and the hi-hat. Count as you like, or as follows: Count 1 A 2 A 3 A 4 A 1 A 2 A 3 A 4 A:

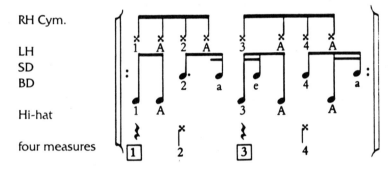

The same rhythm faster. Count as you wish, or as follows. Count: 1 A 2 A 3 A 4 A 1 A 2 A 3 A 4 A. Recorded drummer plays four measure.

Here we have a two-bar pattern consisting of two of the previous rhythmic phrases. Count: 1 A 2–a3 A 4 A 1 A 2–a3e A 4 A:

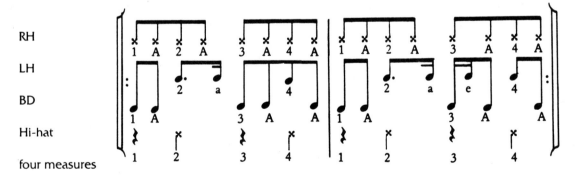

The same rhythm played faster. Count as you wish or as follows. Count: 1 A 2 A 3 A 4 A 1 2 3 4. Recorded drummer plays four measures.

End of Band 16.

BAND 17: Before playing the next two-bar pattern in full, both bars, first practice the second bar by itself, separate from the first bar. ("Bar" and "measures" are used interchangeably here.) Count: 1 A 2–a3e Aa4 A 1 A 2–a3e A a 4 A:

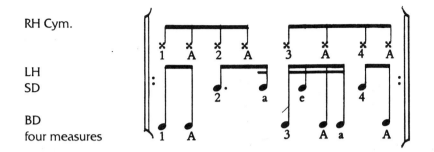

The same rhythm in a faster tempo. Count: 1 A 2 A 3 A 4 A 1 A 2 A 3 A 4 A. Recorded drummer plays four measures.

Now let's play the entire two-bar pattern. Count: 1 A 2–a3e A 4 A:
1 A 2–a3e Aa4 A:

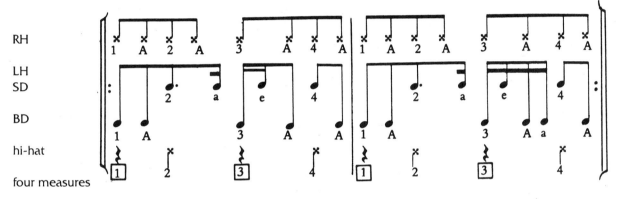

The same rhythm played faster. Count 1 A 2 A 3 A 4 A 1 A 2 A 3 A 4 A. Recorded drummer plays four measures.

The following is a four-measure pattern made up of some of the previous bass drums and left hand rhythms. Count: 1 A 2 A 3 A 4 A 1 A 2 A 3 A 4 A:

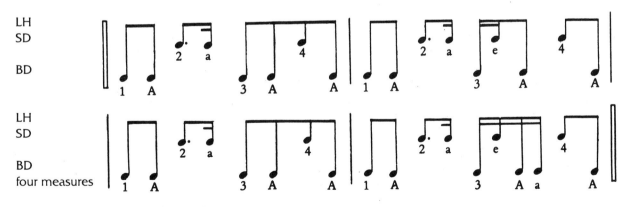

The same rhythm played faster. Count: 1 A 2 A 3 A 4 A 1 A 2 A 3 A 4 A. Recorded drummer plays four measures.

Add the cymbal and hi-hat (to the same rhythm). Count: 1 A 2 A 3 A 4 A 1 A 2 A 3 A 4 A. Recorded drummer plays four measures.

The same four-bar rhythm played faster. Count: 1 A 2 A 3 A 4 A 1 A 2 A 3 A 4 A.

End of Band 17.

BAND 18: Because of their complexity, the preceding rhythms will now be practiced with the group, minus the recorded drummer, in a very slow tempo. Then, when the at-home drummer becomes proficient in playing these rhythms slowly, he will practice them with the faster music in this album. Count: 1 2 3 4.

Recorded group plays sixteen measures – fifteen measures and one beat exactly.
End of Band 18.

BAND 19: THE SHUFFLE RHYTHM: The dotted-eight and sixteenth cymbal rhythm. Count: 1 a 2 a 3 a 4 a 1 a 2 a 3 a 4 a:

RH Cym.
two measures

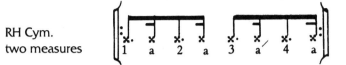

The same cymbal rhythm with the snare drum, bass drum, and hi-hat. Count: 1 a 2 a 3 a 4 a 1 a 2 a 3 a 4 a:

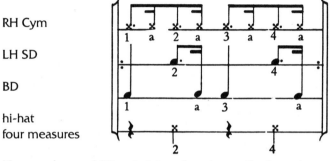

Here we have additional sixteenth notes on the bass drum. Count 1 a 2 a 3 a 4 a 1 a 2 a 3 a 4 a:

The at-home drummer may play the following rhythm with the recorded group – the same rhythm used by the recorded drummer.

The group now plays a slow shuffle, twelve bars with drums; twelve bars minus drums. Stick count-off on 1 2 3 4:

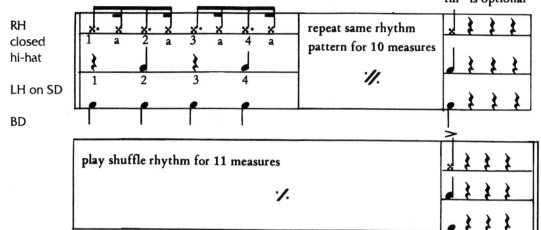

"fill" is optional

The group plays the same format in a faster tempo. Stick count-off on 1 2 3 4. (Same format as shown above.)   End of Band 19.

BAND 20: THE TRIPLET OR TWELVE/EIGHTH FEEL: Sometimes called the gospel type beat.

The following rhythms may be counted in several ways. For example, they may be thought of as being eighth-note triplets in four-four time - one-trip-let two-trip-let three-trip-let four-trip-let; or they may be counted as regular eighths in twelve/eighth time, 1 2 3 4 5 6 7 8 9 10 11 12, and so forth.

First the cymbals rhythm. Count: one trip let two trip let three trip let four trip let 1 2 3 4 5 6 7 8 9 10 11 12:

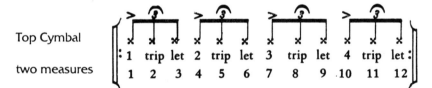

The bass drum and hi-hat rhythm. Count: one–two trip let three–four trip let boom–chick boom boom boom chick–boom boom:

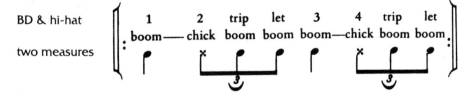

The cymbal, snare, bass drum, and hi-hat combined. The snare drum plays the same rhythm as the hi-hat (on 2 and 4). Count: One trip let two trip let three trip let four trip let:

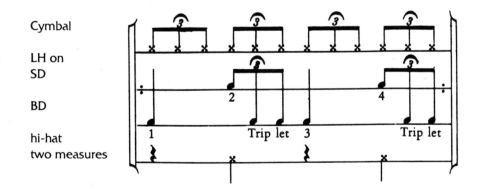

Here we have the same snare, bass and hi-hat rhythm with a variation of the cymbal rhythm, as follows: Count one trip let two trip let three trip let four trip let:

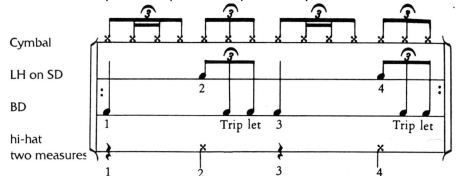

The same rhythm played faster. Here is the tempo: Count: 1 2 3 4 5 6 1 2 3 4 5 6 1 2 3 4 5 6 1 2 3 4 5 6. (Here we counted 1 to 6 four times rather than in triplets or in 12/8 because of the rapidity of the tempo. In the fast tempo, it is verbally easier to count 1 to 6 than in triplets or 12/8.) Recorded drummer plays two measures.

Once again the group plays – first with the recorded drummer, then minus the drums. Note: This time the recorded drummer does not count off the tempo of the music. Instead, the organ plays the pick-up, leading the group into the tune.

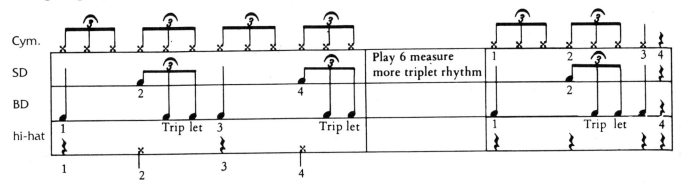

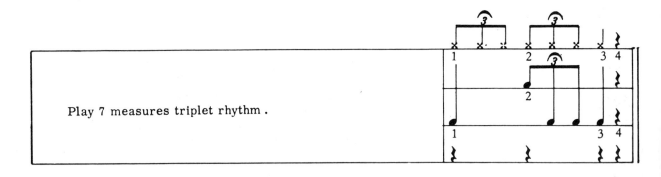

The group now plays in a faster tempo. Follow same format.

Note: The at-home drummer may play the written triplet rhythm pattern, or he may play the variations of that rhythm played by the recorded drummer.

BAND 21: Here we have an exciting piece featuring Mike Ricciardella, the recorded drummer, with the group.

MUSIC MINUS ONE 50 Executive Boulevard • Elmsford, New York 10523-1325